BELLE SOLUTIONS LLC

The
Quick
Flip Blueprint

Turn Fixer-Uppers into Cash

Welcome to Fix-and-Flip Investing

Purpose

Welcome to the world of fix-and-flip investing! In this book, we'll guide you step-by-step through the process of buying, renovating, and selling single-family homes for profit. Whether you're completely new to real estate or have some experience, our goal is to make this approach clear and accessible. By the end, you'll have the confidence and knowledge to start your own fix-and-flip journey.

What is Fix-and-Flip Investing?

Fix-and-flip investing is all about buying a property that needs work, fixing it up, and then selling it for a profit. It's a fast-paced strategy that's great if you're looking to make a good return within a few months, rather than holding onto a property long-term.

You don't need to have a ton of experience to start flipping houses, but you do need the right knowledge, the right strategy, and the right team. That's where this ebook comes in.

Why Fix-and-Flips?

Fixing and flipping homes can be a game-changer when done right. Here's why:

- Fast Profit: You can make a profit in as little as 3 to 6 months if you manage your project well.
- Low Barrier to Entry: You don't need to start with a lot of your own money, especially if you know how to leverage funding (we'll cover that).

- Learning Opportunity: You can quickly gain experience, learning how to identify good deals and manage a rehab project.

What You'll Learn in This Ebook

This ebook will walk you through everything you need to know to successfully flip your first property. Here's what we'll cover:

1. How to Find Good Fix-and-Flip Deals: The best ways to locate homes that are worth flipping.

2. How to Analyze Deals with the 75% Rule: We'll show you exactly how to calculate your offer price so you can ensure a profit.
3. How to Get Funding for Your Flip: Whether you need private money or hard money, we'll explain how to get your deal funded.
4. Managing Your Rehab Project: From contractors to materials, we'll teach you how to stay on budget and on time.
5. How to Sell Your Flip for Maximum Profit: Learn how to price, market, and sell your flip quickly.

Step 1: Understanding the 75% Rule for Fix-and-Flips

Purpose:

In this step, we break down the 75% Rule, a crucial tool that will help you figure out exactly how much to pay for a property so you can make a profit after all the repairs and selling costs.

What is the 75% Rule?

The 75% Rule is a simple formula to help you decide the most you should offer on a property. This rule ensures you'll have a profit margin after you've paid for the property, fixed it up, and sold it. Here's how it works:

You should never pay more than 75% of the property's After Repair Value (ARV) minus the cost of repairs.

Breaking it Down:

- After Repair Value (ARV): This is the amount the house will be worth once it's fully fixed up. You can figure this out by looking at what similar homes in the area (comps) have recently sold for.
- Repair Costs: This is the total cost to fix up the property. This includes everything from new flooring and paint to bigger repairs like a new roof or plumbing.

The 75% Rule Formula:

{Maximum Offer Price} = {ARV} times 0.75) - {Repair Costs}

By following this rule, you protect yourself from overpaying and leave room for profit.

Example:

Let's say you find a property where the After Repair Value (ARV) is $200,000, and the estimated cost to repair the property is $50,000.

Using the 75% rule, you would calculate:

{Maximum Offer Price} = (200,000 times 0.75) - 50,000
{Maximum Offer Price} = 150,000 - 50,000 = 100,000

This means you should not offer more than $100,000 to buy this property.

Why the 75% Rule Works:

By following this rule, you're ensuring that even after paying for repairs and selling costs, there will still be enough money left over for you to make a profit. It also gives you room to cover any unexpected expenses that might come up during the rehab process.

Practice Time:

Start practicing the 75% Rule by looking at properties in your area. Figure out what their ARV would be and estimate repair costs. You can use websites like Zillow or Redfin to find comparable home sales in the area to help with the ARV. The more you practice, the more confident you'll become at analyzing deals.

What's Next?

Now that you understand the 75% Rule, you're ready to start finding properties to flip. In the next section, we'll dive into the best strategies for finding great fix-and-flip deals.

Step 2: Finding Fix-and-Flip Deals

In this step, we'll break down the best strategies for finding profitable fix-and-flip deals. Knowing where to look is key to getting a property below market value, leaving you with enough margin to make a profit after repairs.

1. Local Facebook Communities (Columbus Example)

If you're in the Columbus area, we highly recommend joining the **CREAM Group (Columbus Real Estate and Money)** on Facebook. This is a great resource for finding off-market deals, networking with other real estate investors, and even connecting with people who might have funding options like private money.

For those in other cities:

Each city typically has its own local real estate investing communities on Facebook. Search for groups like "Real Estate Investing in [Your City]" or "[Your City] Off-Market Properties" to find a similar resource where you can network and find deals. These groups are often full of motivated sellers, wholesalers, and real estate agents posting exclusive deals that never hit the MLS (Multiple Listing Service).

2. Driving for Dollars

One of the easiest and most cost-effective ways to find potential flips is by **Driving for Dollars**. This simply means driving around neighborhoods where you want to invest, looking for homes that seem to be neglected or in disrepair. These might be perfect candidates for a fix-and-flip because the owners are often willing to sell at a discount.

What to look for:

- Overgrown lawns or landscaping
- Boarded-up windows or peeling paint
- Notices on the door (foreclosure, tax liens, etc.)
- Homes that appear vacant or abandoned

Once you've identified a few properties, use public records or tools like **PropStream** to find the owner's information and reach out to see if they're interested in selling.

3. Working with Wholesalers

Wholesalers are individuals who find properties at a discount and sell them to investors like you, often for a small fee. They do all the legwork of finding motivated sellers, so you don't have to.

How to connect with wholesalers:

- Network in local real estate groups (like the CREAM group or local meetups).
- Search online for local wholesalers in your area or websites like **BiggerPockets**.
- Let wholesalers know what kind of properties you're looking for, and they'll bring deals directly to you.

4. MLS and Pocket Listings

While most fix-and-flippers try to avoid the MLS (because competition is high), you can still find good deals here, especially if the property has been sitting for a while and the seller is getting desperate.

Pocket listings are properties that agents know are coming to market but haven't been officially listed yet. These can be great opportunities to snag a deal before it's exposed to the public.

How to get MLS and pocket deals:

- Work with a real estate agent who understands fix-and-flip investing and can keep an eye out for distressed properties.
- Let agents know you're interested in pocket listings for homes that need work.

5. Auctions and Foreclosures

Foreclosure auctions can be an excellent place to find deals, but they come with risks. You'll need to have cash on hand and may not be able to inspect the property beforehand, so there's a bit of a gamble involved.

Key things to know:

- Research auction properties ahead of time by visiting foreclosure listing sites.
- Make sure you understand the rules for bidding and have enough cash or funding to close quickly if you win the auction.
- Always run your numbers using the **75% Rule** to make sure you're not overpaying.

6. Direct Mail Campaigns

Another effective strategy is sending **direct mail** to property owners who might be motivated to sell. You can target:

- Out-of-state owners
- Owners of vacant properties
- Owners behind on taxes or mortgage payments

Your mail should offer to buy their house for cash, quickly, and as-is, which can be appealing to people who are in tough situations. This takes a little time and money but can lead to great deals, especially if you focus on specific neighborhoods.

7. Networking with Contractors and Inspectors

Sometimes contractors, inspectors, or even property managers know about deals before they hit the market. These professionals often hear about properties in need of work because they're hired to fix them or assess them for a sale.

How to leverage these contacts:

- Build relationships with local contractors and inspectors by attending real estate investor meetups.
- Let them know you're always looking for properties that need repairs. They might give you a heads-up if they hear about a homeowner looking to sell.

Next Steps:

Once you start finding potential deals, the next step is to **evaluate them using the 75% Rule** and make sure the numbers work before moving forward. We'll dive into how to run those numbers in the next chapter.

Step 3: Evaluating a Fix-and-Flip Deal

Now that you've got some strategies for finding potential deals, it's time to evaluate them. Not every property is a good candidate for a fix-and-flip, so knowing how to crunch the numbers is essential. In this chapter, we'll go step-by-step through how to evaluate a property to make sure it's a solid investment.

Step 1: Determine the After Repair Value (ARV)

The After Repair Value (ARV) is the most important number when evaluating a fix-and-flip. It's what the property will be worth after you've completed all the repairs. To figure this out, you need to look at comparable properties (comps) that have recently sold in the same area and are similar to the property you're looking at. (Step 1: Understanding the 75% Rule for Fix-andFlips)

Step 2: Walk the Property with a General Contractor (GC)

When evaluating a potential fix-and-flip property, it's highly recommended to bring a General Contractor (GC) with you during the walkthrough. A GC will help you assess the property's condition, point out hidden repair needs, and give you a more accurate estimate of the rehab costs.

Why Bring a GC?

- Professional Insight: They'll catch things you might miss, like structural issues, plumbing, or electrical problems.
- Accurate Estimates: GCs can give you on-the-spot estimates for repairs, helping you avoid underestimating costs.
- Future Relationship: Establishing a relationship with a reliable GC early can streamline future projects, as they become familiar with your expectations and goals.

How to Find a Reliable GC:

1. **Ask for Referrals:**

Reach out to other investors in your local community (e.g., Columbus Real Estate and Money Group on Facebook or other local investing groups) to get recommendations. Networking with other flippers can help you connect with experienced GCs who specialize in fix-and-flips.

2. Search Online Platforms:

Use websites like Angi (formerly Angie's List), HomeAdvisor, or Thumbtack to find well-reviewed contractors in your area. Be sure to read reviews, check their portfolio of work, and schedule an interview.

3. Local Real Estate Meetups:

Attend local real estate investor meetups where contractors often network with investors. You'll find that many contractors already have experience working on fix-and-flip projects, which can save you time and hassle.

4. Ask for Quotes:

Once you've narrowed down a few options, have each GC walk the property and provide you with a detailed quote for the repairs. This will also give you a better idea of who you'd prefer to work with long-term.

Sometimes, property owners may prefer not to deal with multiple showings, and that's perfectly fine. In such cases, it's advisable to bring at least one general contractor (GC) with you during your initial walk-through.

Step 3: Estimate the Repair Costs

After walking the property with a GC, you'll have a clear estimate of the repair costs. This includes everything from minor cosmetic repairs like paint and flooring to major issues like plumbing or a new roof.

Key Tip: Make sure your GC gives you a written estimate to ensure there's a clear understanding of the project scope and budget.

Common Repair Costs:

- Cosmetic Repairs (paint, flooring, etc.): $10,000 - $20,000
- Kitchen Remodel: $10,000 - $30,000
- Bathroom Remodel: $5,000 - $15,000
- Roof Replacement: $5,000 - $10,000
- Plumbing or Electrical Work: $5,000 - $15,000

Tip: It's always better to overestimate repair costs than underestimate. You want to make sure there's enough room in your budget for unexpected expenses.

Step 4: Apply the 75% Rule

Now that you know the ARV and estimated repair costs, you can use the 75% Rule to figure out the maximum amount you should offer on the property.

Formula Recap:

{Maximum Offer Price} = {ARV} times 0.75) - {Repair Costs}

Example:

Let's continue with the example from above:

- ARV: $250,000
- Repair Costs: $40,000

{Maximum Offer Price} = (250,000 times 0.75) - 40,000

{Maximum Offer Price} = 187,500 - 40,000 = 147,500

So, the most you should offer on this property is $147,500. This ensures that after repairs and selling costs, you'll still have a profit margin.

Step 5: Calculate Holding and Selling Costs

In addition to repair costs, you need to account for holding costs and selling costs. These are the expenses you'll have while you own the property and when you eventually sell it.

Holding Costs Include:

- Mortgage Payments
- Property Taxes
- Utilities
- Insurance

Selling Costs Include:

- Realtor Commissions (typically 5-6%)
- Closing Costs
- Title Insurance

Step 6: Run the Final Numbers

Now that you know the purchase price, repair costs, holding costs, and selling costs, you can calculate your potential profit.

Formula:

{Profit} = {ARV} - ({Purchase Price} + {Repair Costs} + {Holding Costs} + {Selling Costs})

Example:

- ARV: $250,000
- Purchase Price: $147,500
- Repair Costs: $40,000
- Holding Costs: $6,000
- Selling Costs: $15,000

{Profit} = 250,000 - (147,500 + 40,000 + 6,000 + 15,000)

{Profit} = 250,000 - 208,500 = 41,500

So, if everything goes according to plan, you'll make a $41,500 profit on this deal. If the numbers don't work, move on to the next deal.

Step 7: Backup Plan

Always have a backup plan. Markets change, and sometimes repairs cost more than expected. If you can't sell for the price you hoped, consider holding the property as a rental until the market improves. Keep this in mind when evaluating your deals.

Next Steps:

Now that you know how to evaluate a deal and work with a GC to get repair estimates, you're ready to make offers. In the next section, we'll cover how to get funding for your fix-and-flip projects.

Step 4: Getting Funding for Your Fix-and-Flip

Now that you know how to find and evaluate deals, the next crucial step is securing funding to make it all happen. Whether you're using your own money, tapping into private lenders, or leveraging hard money loans, having the right funding strategy is key to successfully completing your flip.

1. Belle Solutions: Your First Funding Option

At **Belle Solutions**, we offer hard money lending to help you get your fix-and-flip projects off the ground. Our lending partners offer a loan structure designed to be flexible and investor-friendly, with us acting as your broker to help secure the best terms:

- **Up to 90% of the Purchase Price:** Our lender will cover up to 90% of the property purchase, allowing you to keep more cash on hand.
- **100% of Rehab Costs:** Our lender will fund the entire rehab, so you can focus on getting the work done without worrying about out-of-pocket repair costs.

How to Apply:

If you've found a deal that meets the 75% Rule and are ready to move forward, we'd love to help fund your project. Belle Solutions Loan Application to submit your deal to Belle Solutions for review, and we'll get back to you with the next steps.

This option gives you fast, reliable funding without the hassle of traditional banks, and our team is here to support you through the entire flip process.

2. Private Money Lenders

Another great option for funding your flip is **private money lenders**. These are individuals (often other investors) who lend money to fund real estate deals, usually in exchange for a fixed return or a percentage of the profits.

How to Find Private Money Lenders:

- **Local Real Estate Meetups:** Attend events in your area where private lenders network with investors. You'll find people who are looking to make a return on their capital by funding fix-and-flip projects.
- **Online Real Estate Forums:** Websites like **BiggerPockets** or Facebook groups (like the CREAM group) are great places to connect with private lenders.
- **Friends and Family:** Sometimes, your personal network can be a great resource for private money. They may be more willing to invest in your project if you show them the numbers and a clear plan for repayment.

Terms to Expect:

Private money terms vary but expect to pay interest rates between **8-12%** annually, with loan terms ranging from **6-12 months**. Some private lenders may also require a small percentage of the profit when the deal closes.

3. Traditional Hard Money Loans

If you can't secure funding through Belle Solutions or private lenders, you can always look into other **hard money lenders**. These are specialized lenders that provide short-term loans for real estate investments, especially fix-and-flips.

Pros of Hard Money:

- **Fast Approval:** Hard money loans are typically approved within days, not weeks like traditional banks.
- **Flexible Terms:** Many hard money lenders offer flexible terms that can fit your deal's specific needs.

Cons of Hard Money:

- **Higher Interest Rates:** Expect rates around **10-15%**, which is higher than conventional loans.
- **Points and Fees:** Hard money lenders often charge points (fees) upfront, which can range from **2-5% of the loan amount**.

How to Find a Hard Money Lender:

- **Referrals:** Ask other investors or contractors for recommendations on reliable hard money lenders.
- **Online Searches:** Websites like **LendingHome** or **Fund That Flip** can connect you with national hard money lenders.

4. Using Your Own Cash

If you have the funds available, you may want to consider using your own cash for the deal. While this method gives you the most control, it also ties up your money, leaving less available for future investments.

Advantages:

- **No Loan Payments:** You won't have to pay interest or fees on your own money, maximizing your profit.
- **Complete Control:** You'll have full control over the deal without having to meet lender requirements or timelines.

Disadvantages:

- **Cash is Tied Up:** If all your money is tied up in one deal, it limits your ability to take on other projects or cover unexpected costs.

Next Steps:

Now that you have a clear understanding of the different funding options, you're ready to get the money you need to fund your fix-and-flip project. Remember, **Belle Solutions** is your first option for fast, investor-friendly funding. Belle Solutions Loan Application to submit your deal, and let's get started!

In the next chapter, we'll dive into **how to manage your rehab** and make sure you stay on budget and on time.

Step 5: Managing Your Rehab Project

Once you've secured funding for your fix-and-flip, the next critical step is managing the rehab process. This is where many new investors can go off track, so it's important to have a solid plan in place to stay on budget and on schedule. In this section, we'll walk you through how to manage your rehab project effectively.

Step 1: Create a Detailed Rehab Plan

Before any work begins, create a detailed rehab plan that outlines everything that needs to be done. This plan will help keep you organized and give your contractors a clear direction.

Key Elements of a Rehab Plan:

- **Scope of Work:** List out every repair or upgrade you'll need, from cosmetic changes like paint and flooring to major repairs like plumbing or electrical work.
- **Timeline:** Create a timeline that shows when each task will be completed. Work with your contractor to set realistic deadlines.
- **Budget:** Make sure every line item in the scope of work has an estimated cost attached to it. Include a 10-20% contingency fund for unexpected expenses.

Bonus:

To make this process easier, we're providing a **blank Scope of Work** template in PDF format that you can fill out for your own projects.

Step 2: Hire Reliable Contractors

Hiring the right contractors is one of the most important steps in the rehab process. You want to work with professionals who are reliable, experienced, and budget-conscious.

How to Find Contractors:

- **Ask for Referrals:** Start by asking other investors or real estate professionals for contractor recommendations. They can give you insight into contractors who understand the fix-and-flip business.

- **Interview Multiple Contractors:** Don't go with the first contractor you meet. Get multiple quotes, compare prices, and make sure each contractor is licensed and insured.
- **Check References:** Always ask contractors for references from past clients. This gives you a chance to hear how they handled previous projects, including budget and timeline management.

Step 3: Set Clear Expectations

Once you've hired your contractors, it's important to set clear expectations from the start. This includes everything from how often you'll communicate to how you'll handle changes to the plan.

Key Points to Discuss:

- **Communication:** Decide on regular check-ins, whether daily or weekly, to ensure the project is moving forward.
- **Budget & Payments:** Outline the payment structure upfront. Avoid paying too much upfront, and set milestone payments based on completed work.
- **Change Orders:** Establish a process for any changes to the rehab plan. If the contractor finds unexpected problems, have a system in place for approving or denying additional costs.

Step 4: Track Your Expenses

One of the most common mistakes in fix-and-flips is not keeping track of expenses. From materials to labor, every dollar spent needs to be accounted for. Staying on top of your expenses helps ensure you don't go over budget.

Tools to Help You Track Expenses:

- **Google Sheets or Excel:** Create a simple spreadsheet where you track each line item and its cost.

- **Contractor Invoices:** Keep all contractor invoices organized and review them regularly to ensure they match the work completed.
- **Receipts for Materials:** Save all receipts for materials and supplies, and compare them against your original budget estimates.

Step 5: Monitor the Progress

As the project progresses, make regular visits to the property to ensure that the work is being done as expected. This will help you spot potential issues early before they become expensive problems.

What to Look For During Site Visits:

- **Work Quality:** Make sure the contractors are meeting your quality standards. Look out for sloppy work or corners being cut.
- **Progress vs. Timeline:** Check to see if the project is staying on schedule. If delays are happening, discuss ways to get the project back on track.
- **Budget:** Compare the actual work done to the budgeted costs. If costs are rising, make adjustments where possible to avoid going over budget.

Step 6: Final Walkthrough

Once the rehab is complete, do a final walkthrough with your contractor. Use this as an opportunity to catch any last-minute issues or touch-ups that need to be done before you list the property for sale.

Checklist for the Final Walkthrough:

- **Check All Repairs:** Make sure every item on the original rehab plan has been completed to your satisfaction.

- **Test All Systems:** Check the plumbing, electrical, HVAC, and appliances to ensure they're working correctly.
- **Cosmetic Touches:** Look for any missed cosmetic details like paint touch-ups, missing trim, or unclean areas.

Next Steps:

Once your rehab is complete, you're ready for the final phase of your fix-and-flip: **Selling the Property**. In the next section, we'll dive into how to price, market, and sell your flip quickly to maximize your profits.

Step 6: Selling Your Fix-and-Flip Property

Congratulations! You've successfully completed the rehab, and now it's time for the final step—selling the property and cashing in on your hard work. In this section, we'll walk you through how to price, market, and sell your flip quickly and for maximum profit.

Step 1: Set the Right Price

Pricing your flip correctly is key to selling it fast and maximizing your profit. If you price it too high, the property could sit on the market for months, racking up holding costs. Price it too low, and you're leaving money on the table.

How to Determine the Best Price:

- **Use Recent Comps:** Look at recent sales of similar homes in the same neighborhood (within the last 3-6 months). Focus on properties with the same number of bedrooms, bathrooms, and square footage.
- **Consider the Market Conditions:** If the market is hot, you might be able to price slightly higher, but if it's slow, be conservative with your pricing.
- **Consult with Your Real Estate Agent:** A great real estate agent will know the local market trends and help you set a competitive price.

Step 2: Hire the Right Selling Agent

For first-time flippers, having a real estate agent who truly understands the fix-and-flip process can make a huge difference. That's why we highly recommend working with **Kristina Belle**, an expert real estate agent who specializes in selling flipped properties.

Why Work with Kristina Belle?

- **Experience with Fix-and-Flips:** Kristina has a deep understanding of the fix-and-flip process and knows exactly how to market and sell these types of properties for top dollar.
- **Expert Pricing Strategy:** She will help you set a competitive price based on market conditions and comparable properties.
- **Connections with Buyers:** Kristina has a network of buyers who are often looking for newly renovated properties, which can help you sell faster.
- **Staging and Presentation:** She knows how to present a flip in the best light to make it appealing to buyers, from staging tips to professional photography.

- If you're in the Columbus area, Kristina Belle is the perfect agent to help you sell your flip.

If you're outside the Columbus market and looking to sell your fix-and-flip property, finding the right real estate agent is essential to ensure a smooth and profitable sale. Not all agents are equipped to handle investment properties, so it's important to choose someone with the right expertise. Follow these steps to find a qualified agent who can help you maximize your returns and successfully sell your property.

1. Find a Local Expert

- Choose a real estate agent with extensive knowledge of your specific market and neighborhood to ensure they understand local trends and pricing.

2. Look for Experience with Fix-and-Flips

- Select an agent who has experience selling renovated homes and understands how to market the improvements you've made.

3. Interview and Compare Agents

- Meet with several agents, review their marketing strategies, and check their references to ensure they have a strong track record.

4. Assess Their Network

- Opt for an agent with a broad network of buyers and industry professionals, increasing the chances of a faster sale.

5. Ensure Clear Communication

- Choose an agent who is responsive and proactive, keeping you informed and involved throughout the selling process.

Step 3: Stage the Property

Staging is one of the most effective ways to attract buyers and get higher offers. A well-staged home helps buyers envision themselves living in the space, and it highlights the property's best features.

Simple Staging Tips:

- **Clean and Declutter:** Make sure the home is spotless and remove any personal items or unnecessary clutter.
- **Use Neutral Decor:** Stick to neutral colors for furniture, artwork, and accessories. You want the home to appeal to as many buyers as possible.
- **Highlight Key Areas:** Focus on staging the living room, kitchen, and master bedroom. These are the spaces buyers care about the most.
- **Curb Appeal:** Don't forget the outside of the house! Make sure the lawn is mowed, bushes are trimmed, and the front door looks inviting.

Step 4: Market Your Property

Marketing is critical to getting your flip in front of the right buyers. Your real estate agent will handle most of this, but here's what to expect:

Marketing Strategies:

- **Online Listings:** Your home will be listed on the MLS and popular real estate websites like Zillow, Redfin, and Realtor.com.

- **Professional Photos:** High-quality photos are essential to showcase your flip in the best light. Many buyers start their home search online, so good photos can make all the difference.
- **Open Houses:** Your agent may host open houses or private showings to generate interest and get buyers through the door.
- **Social Media Promotion:** A strong social media presence can drive more attention to your property. Share the listing on Facebook, Instagram, and real estate groups to reach a wider audience.

Step 5: Negotiate the Best Offer

Once offers start coming in, it's time to negotiate. This is where your real estate agent will help you get the best possible deal.

Things to Consider When Negotiating:

- **Offer Price:** Look at the buyer's offer and compare it to your asking price and recent comps. If it's close, you might want to accept it or counter with a slightly higher number.
- **Contingencies:** Be mindful of any contingencies in the offer, such as inspection or financing conditions. Contingencies can delay closing, so consider offers with fewer contingencies if you're looking to sell quickly.
- **Closing Timeline:** Some buyers may want a quick closing, while others may need more time. Be flexible, but also consider how long you're willing to hold the property before selling.

Step 6: Close the Deal

Once you've accepted an offer and the buyer's financing and inspections are in order, you're ready to close the deal! At closing, you'll sign the paperwork, the buyer will transfer the funds, and you'll officially sell the property.

What to Expect at Closing:

- **Final Walkthrough:** The buyer will do a final walkthrough of the property to ensure everything is in good condition.
- **Signing Documents:** You'll sign the necessary paperwork to transfer ownership of the property to the buyer.
- **Receiving Payment:** Once everything is signed, you'll receive your payment. Congratulations—you've successfully completed your fix-and-flip!

Next Steps:

With your first fix-and-flip complete, you're ready to move on to the next project! In the final chapter, we'll discuss how to build momentum, scale your fix-and-flip business, and continue growing as a real estate investor.

Key Team Members to Consider:

- **Real Estate Agents:** You'll need agents who understand the market and can help you find off-market deals and sell properties quickly.
- **General Contractors (GCs):** A good GC is crucial to completing your rehabs on time and on budget. Once you've built a strong relationship, your GC can handle multiple properties simultaneously.
- **Private Money Lenders:** Build a network of private money lenders who are interested in funding your deals. The more options you have, the easier it will be to secure funding quickly.
- **Wholesalers:** Establish relationships with wholesalers who can bring you a steady flow of off-market deals.

- **Stagers and Photographers:** These professionals can help you sell properties faster by making them look their best online and in person.

By assembling a reliable team, you can delegate tasks and focus on the bigger picture—finding more deals and expanding your business.

Step 3: Manage Multiple Projects

As you start taking on more than one flip at a time, organization becomes even more important. You'll need to track multiple timelines, budgets, and teams across several properties.

How to Manage Multiple Projects:

- **Use Project Management Tools:** Consider using tools like **Google Sheets**, **Trello**, or **Asana** to keep track of each property's progress, budgets, and timelines. These tools allow you to set deadlines, assign tasks, and monitor progress in real time.
- **Set Up Regular Check-ins:** Schedule weekly check-ins with your team, including contractors, real estate agents, and project managers. This ensures that everyone is on the same page and that any issues are addressed quickly.
- **Outsource Where Possible:** Consider outsourcing tasks like bookkeeping, marketing, or even deal evaluation to free up your time for more important activities like finding deals or managing relationships.

With the right systems and tools in place, you'll be able to scale your fix-and-flip business without getting overwhelmed.

Step 4: Expand Your Deal Sources

To scale, you'll need a constant flow of deals. Relying on just one or two sources won't be enough if you want to grow. Here are a few ways to expand your deal sources:

Expanding Your Deal Sources:

- **Wholesalers:** Continue building relationships with multiple wholesalers who can bring you off-market deals.
- **Direct Mail Campaigns:** Ramp up your direct mail campaigns targeting distressed property owners, out-of-state landlords, or those facing foreclosure.
- **Networking:** Attend local real estate meetups, join Facebook groups (like the **CREAM group**), and stay active in your local investor community to hear about upcoming deals.
- **Auctions and Foreclosures:** Keep an eye on foreclosure auctions or distressed property auctions in your area. These can be great places to find deals if you're prepared to act quickly.
- **Online Tools:** Use online platforms like PropStream, Zillow, or Redfin to find motivated sellers or pre-foreclosure properties.

The more sources you have, the more opportunities you'll find. Having multiple deal sources ensures that your pipeline stays full, even as you scale up your business.

Step 5: Leverage Other Investors

As your business grows, consider partnering with other investors to take on bigger or riskier projects. You can split the investment, reduce your risk, and potentially take on multiple large projects at once.

Ways to Partner with Other Investors:

- **Joint Ventures:** Partner with another investor to pool your resources and take on larger deals that you might not be able to handle alone.
- **Private Money Partnerships:** Work with private money lenders who can fund larger projects in exchange for a percentage of the profits.
- **Flip and Hold Partnerships:** If you prefer flipping but want to diversify, consider partnering with investors who focus on rental properties. You can handle the rehab and sale, while they manage the long-term hold.

By leveraging other investors, you can grow your portfolio and increase your profits without taking on all the risk yourself.

Next Steps:

Scaling your fix-and-flip business is all about creating systems, building a strong team, and expanding your deal sources. As you continue to grow, you'll find more opportunities to take on bigger projects and make larger profits. Remember, the key to long-term success is staying organized, managing your team effectively, and always keeping an eye out for new deals.

About Us and Our Mission

Belle Solutions, led by husband-and-wife team Andre and Kristina Belle, is a trusted name in real estate investing with a primary focus on fix-and-flip projects. With years of experience in the industry, the Belles have successfully transformed distressed properties into profitable investments, building a reputation for excellence and expertise in every deal.

Andre Belle brings his entrepreneurial skills from years of building successful businesses, while Kristina, a licensed real estate agent, combines her market knowledge with hands-on experience in project management. Together, they offer a comprehensive approach to real estate investing, from finding properties to renovation and resale.

Belle Solutions is committed to helping clients achieve success in their fix-and-flip ventures, offering mentorship, guidance, and a wealth of industry insights to new and experienced investors alike. Whether you're looking to get started in real estate or need a seasoned team to help you flip properties, Belle Solutions provides the expertise and support to make it happen.

www.ingramcontent.com/pod-product-compliance
Lightning Source LLC
Chambersburg PA
CBHW040338220526
45473CB00009B/2726